The Chernobyl Disaster

PERSPECTIVES ON

The Chernobyl Disaster

Legacy and Impact on the Future of Nuclear Energy

WIL MARA

mc **Marshall Cavendish**
Benchmark
New York

Other Marshall Cavendish Offices: Marshall Cavendish International (Asia) Private Limited, 1 New Industrial Road, Singapore 536196 • Marshall Cavendish International (Thailand) Co Ltd. 253 Asoke, 12th Flr, Sukhumvit 21 Road, Klongtoey Nua, Wattana, Bangkok 10110, Thailand • Marshall Cavendish (Malaysia) Sdn Bhd, Times Subang, Lot 46, Subang Hi-Tech Industrial Park, Batu Tiga, 40000 Shah Alam, Selangor Darul Ehsan, Malaysia

Marshall Cavendish is a trademark of Times Publishing Limited

All websites were available and accurate when this book was sent to press.

Library of Congress Cataloging-in-Publication Data

Mara, Wil.
The Chernobyl disaster : legacy and impact on the future of nuclear energy / by Wil Mara.
p. cm. — (Perspectives on)
Summary: "Provides comprehensive information on the nuclear disaster at the Chernobyl nuclear power plant and the differing perspectives accompanying it"—Provided by publisher.
Includes bibliographical references and index.
ISBN 978-0-7614-4984-3
1. Chernobyl Nuclear Accident, Chernobyl, Ukraine, 1986—Juvenile literature. 2. Radioactive pollution—Juvenile literature. 3. Nuclear accidents—Environmental aspects—Juvenile literature. 4. Nuclear energy—Environmental aspects—Juvenile literature. 5. Nuclear energy—Safety measures—Juvenile literature. I. Title.
TK1362.U38M37 2011
363.17'99094777—dc22
2009048257

Editor: Christine Florie
Publisher: Michelle Bisson
Art Director: Anahid Hamparian
Series Designer: Sonia Chaghatzbanian

Expert Reader: Professor Jason Hayward, Joint Faculty Appointment, University of Tennessee Nuclear Engineering, Oakridge National Laboratory

Photo research by Marybeth Kavanagh

Cover photo by AP Photo

The photographs in this book are used by permission and through the courtesy of:
Corbis: Damir Sagolj (Reuters), 2–3; Gleb Garanich (Reuters), 43; Kostin/Sygma, 30, 47, 58; Sergei Supinsky/epa, 87; *AP Photo*: 8, 55; Rainer Klostermeier, 60; Kurt Strumpf, 78; Carol J. Williams, 89; *Photo Researchers, Inc.*: David Nicholls, 10; SPL, 19; Vaughan Melzer/JVZ, 25, 27; LLNL, 51; *Getty Images*: Norm Betts/Bloomberg, 14; Pierre Mion/National Geographic, 35; NASA (Time Life Pictures), 49; Francois Lochon (Time Life Pictures), 52; Diana Walker(Time Life Pictures), 56; Sergei Supinsky/AFP, 65; Ezra Shaw, 73; *Everett Collection*: Julian Simmonds/Rex USA, 16; *The Image Works*: RIA Novosti/TopFoto, 22, 63, 69, 80, 90; *Reuters*: 28

Printed in Malaysia (T)
1 3 5 6 4 2

Contents

Introduction

ALONG WITH SCORES OF other discoveries and innovations, the twentieth century ushered in the beginning of the atomic age.

The earliest perceived uses for atomic power were military. During World War II (1939–1945) scientists working in the United States built the first nuclear reactor, and from this eventually came the Manhattan Project, which produced a pair of atomic bombs that were dropped on the Japanese cities of Hiroshima and Nagasaki in August 1945 and killed more than 200,000 people. Nuclear energy was first used to create something of everyday value—electricity—in December 1951 at an experimental site in Idaho; the project's first output produced enough electricity to power a handful of lightbulbs.

In the 1970s oil shortages hit the industrialized nations of the world hard, and the price of fossil fuels began to climb. At the start of the 1970s there were only about seventy-five nuclear reactors operating around the world; that number more than doubled by the end of the decade.

The enthusiasm to "go nuclear" waned somewhat in March 1979, when the Three Mile Island nuclear facility, located near Harrisburg, Pennsylvania, suffered a serious accident—a partial core meltdown that resulted in the release of radioactive material into the atmosphere. Some critics of nuclear power consider the Three Mile Island incident a precursor to what happened at the Chernobyl nuclear power plant in the Ukraine just over seven years later.

The Chernobyl accident occurred on April 26, 1986, when one of four reactors at the plant suffered a steam rupture. An ensuing chemical explosion blew apart a vessel containing tons of radioactive material, which was sent into the skies and began a destructive journey around the globe. What was most shocking to people around the world was not that the power of the atom could cause such an accident but that the radioactive material was allowed to escape in the first place. Two plant workers were killed during the explosion. In addition, more than forty people who helped with the initial emergency response died. In the years that followed, thousands more died from various causes, all of which stemmed from the release of radiation at Chernobyl.

Could the Chernobyl nuclear disaster have been avoided? Even with the advantage of hindsight, this question is difficult to answer. Some consider the events of April 1986 to have been nothing more than an unfortunate chapter in the story of man's interaction with nuclear power. Others say it is where the story should have ended altogether.

This book will attempt to examine the Chernobyl disaster, the lessons learned from it, and how those lessons might best be applied in a future where finding new forms of energy will be critical to serving humanity's needs.

One

A Moment in History

THE CHERNOBYL POWER PLANT was built in the Kiev Oblast district of the Ukraine, about 11.2 miles (18 kilometers) northwest of the city of Chernobyl and about 10 miles (16 km) south of the Ukraine's border with Belarus. To fully appreciate the scope of the disaster, you must first gain a basic understanding of how a nuclear plant operates.

Nuclear Plant Basics

Nuclear energy is like any other form of energy in that it can become very difficult to control if concentrated in great amounts. Yet it comes from a very tiny source—the atom. An atom is a particle so small that it cannot be seen without the help of instrumentation, such as a microscope. The atom is one of the most basic forms of matter. It is the most basic part of any of the more than one hundred known elements: oxygen, hydrogen, gold, silver, and so on. The atom consists of a nucleus containing a certain number of neutrons and protons. The exact number of these particles is what determines the

In April 1986 a reactor at the Chernobyl nuclear power plant exploded, emitting radioactive material into the atmosphere. Workers go about their duties (left) in a Chernobyl reactor room four years prior to the accident.

identity of an element. Circling the nucleus are one or more electrons, which are held in place by electromagnetic force. Each element has its own combination of protons, neutrons, and electrons.

Nuclear energy is produced from an atom through one of two processes—fission or fusion. Fission is the splitting of the atom's nucleus, whereas fusion is the merging of one or more nuclei. At the Chernobyl power plant, energy was produced

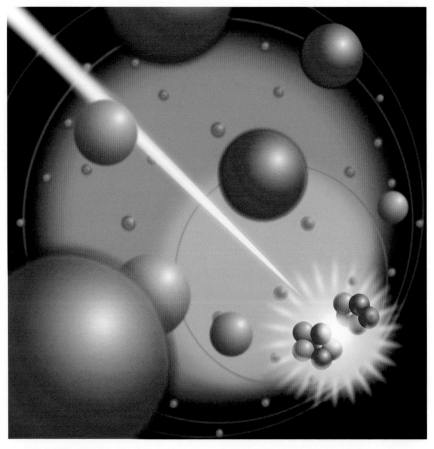

During the fission process, atoms are struck by neutrons, and energy is released.

using the fission process, wherein atoms are bombarded by neutrons. When the bombardment causes an atom to split, a great amount of energy is released.

Since millions of atoms were subjected to the fission process at Chernobyl, the volume of energy produced was enormous. What made this process even more productive is the phenomenon of the chain reaction—when an atom is split, it produces free neutrons that can split more atoms. As long as the workers in the Chernobyl plant added more nuclear fuel—fresh chemical elements, such as uranium— into the fission process, the chain reaction continued.

The purpose of the Chernobyl plant was to produce electricity. However, the energy produced through nuclear fission is not converted directly into electricity—the fission process is just the beginning. Fission occurs inside a container called a reactor core. Fission produces a tremendous amount of heat. This heat is used to boil vast quantities of water, which turn into steam. The steam is then forced through several turbines—rotors with large blades, vaguely similar to airplane propellers. The forced steam causes the turbines to spin, and the spinning produces energy that is then converted into electricity. The electricity is fed through power lines into nearby neighborhoods, where it is then used for everyday electrical needs.

One of the advantages of using nuclear energy to produce electricity is that it releases only very small amounts of greenhouse gases, such as carbon dioxide. In a world where environmentally friendly forms of energy are becoming increasingly important, nuclear energy offers a tremendous benefit. Fully operational nuclear plants cause very little

Uranium 235 — Friend or Foe?

The most commonly used element in the nuclear fission process is uranium, and the most common variant used for this purpose is known as uranium 235 (^{235}U). When bombarded with neutrons, ^{235}U will quickly start a chain reaction that produces tremendous amounts of heat—ideal for nuclear reactors. Uranium 235 was first discovered in 1935 by a Canadian physicist named Arthur Dempster. Although it does not exist in great quantities in nature (less than 1 percent of all uranium atoms are of the 235 variety), it is still extracted, usually from the mineral uraninite (much of which is found in

Canada and Australia), because of its many industrial and military uses. Part of its tremendous value is that 1 pound (0.45 kilograms) of it can produce the same amount of thermal energy as 1,500 tons of coal. One of the unfortunate characteristics of ^{235}U is that it also produces highly radioactive by-products during the fission process. Another is that it has a half-life of roughly 700 million years; that is, it takes 700 million years for half of the radioactive material to become harmless, and it takes the same amount of time for half of the radioactive remainder to become harmless, and so on.

In a nuclear power plant, steam produced from boiling water is forced through turbines like this. The spinning of the blades produces energy that is converted into electricity.

harm to the atmosphere—and dramatically less than power plants running on other forms of energy. Also, a single nuclear power plant is able to produce vast amounts of electricity and in turn can meet the needs of a large geographic area. Thus, a nuclear plant is inherently more efficient than other kinds of power plants.

On the other hand, there are inherent dangers involved in the fission process. One is that it also produces a series of unwanted, radioactive elements. Radioactive elements throw off energy in two forms, particles and waves, both of which can be harmful to living organisms, including humans. The damage can be extensive and unpredictable. Exposure to radiation can cause chronicle illness and even death. Whether this risk of harm is worth taking is central to the nuclear power debate. In his 1986 book *Nuclear Power: Siting and Safety*, Stan Openshaw makes a critical point: "The probability of such a large accident may well be vanishingly small, but the consequences could be so devastating. Additionally, it should be noted that similar low-probability events do occur and, moreover, might well be expected to occur in the immediate future."

Understanding the dangers of radiation is essential to understanding the magnitude of what happened at Chernobyl. If the fission process did not produce any radioactive material, the accident would have been considerably less dramatic.

A Safety Test

The Chernobyl accident began as a safety test. The purpose of the test was to see what would happen to a reactor in the event of an electrical power outage. The main concern was that the core of the reactor would overheat from uncontrolled fission, with a meltdown or an explosion as the possible outcome. Tons of radioactive material would escape and be released not just around the plant but into the general atmosphere as well.

The reactors at Chernobyl had several safety features to prevent such a disaster, but most were controlled electronically and therefore would not function during a power outage. However, even in a blackout, the turbines that

Viktor Bryukhanov, Chernobyl's director in April 1986, initiated the safety test that would ultimately destroy one of the plant's reactors.

produced electricity would continue to spin as a result of momentum. The director of the Chernobyl power plant, Viktor Bryukhanov, wanted to know if this momentum would produce enough electricity to keep the safety features functional. There was only one way to find out for sure: come as close as possible to simulating a real blackout.

Fabricating a power outage at a nuclear power plant had the potential to be a very dangerous endeavor. Was Bryukhanov justified in wanting this test performed? In his 1982 book *Three Mile Island: Thirty Minutes to Meltdown*, Daniel Ford makes a point: "Scientists prefer to see important tests and experiments—especially potentially hazardous ones—performed under carefully controlled conditions. Valuable data are occasionally acquired, however, in unplanned and less than scientific ways." There are reasons to question Bryukhanov's suitability for his job. He received the directorship of the Chernobyl power plant when in his mid-thirties, a young age for the nuclear industry. Also, he had never worked with nuclear power before, his expertise instead being with turbines. Nevertheless, he had impressed several of his superiors through the years and received this very important position.

The details of the test at the Chernobyl plant were planned out by the chief engineer, Nikolai Fomin. When Fomin began working at Chernobyl, he, too, had had no training in the nuclear industry; his experience was in electrical engineering. Fomin was on very good terms with Bryukhanov, and as a result, he was gradually promoted up the ranks until, as chief engineer, he oversaw the day-to-day workings of all four reactors. The plan he designed for the test required that the safety features for reactor #4 and its turbogenerators (generators connected to the turbines) be switched off. Similar test plans had been proposed at other nuclear sites, but the administrators in those locations had rejected them as being too dangerous.

In January 1986 Bryukhanov submitted the Chernobyl plan for approval to four different government organizations. They were supposed to review the plan and give Bryukhanov permission to proceed. None of these organizations gave permission, however. This refusal to give the go-ahead for the planned test did not strike Bryukhanov as unusual. In the Soviet government the safest way for people in positions of responsibility to protect their jobs was to avoid making decisions on delicate matters.

Bryukhanov decided to go ahead with the test without government approval, confident it would be successful in spite of the unstable conditions it would create. The Chernobyl power plant had been running for many years with no major problems; he believed everything was well under control.

Creating the Test Conditions

On April 25, 1986, the first step in creating the desired test conditions began. At 1:00 p.m. the power output of reactor #4 was dropped to about half its normal level—from 3000 megawatts (MW) to 1600 MW. One of the two turbogenerators was switched off; only one was needed for the test.

At 2:00 p.m. the emergency core cooling system (ECCS), the first safety device, was disengaged. The ECCS includes a series of automatic features that shuts down and then treats a reactor during crisis conditions. The ECCS administers the injection of coolants to the reactor to quickly reduce its temperature and also opens valves to release steam should the pressure get too high. Chernobyl's operators shut off the ECCS because they feared it would inject frigid coolants into the white-hot reactor during the test and damage it.

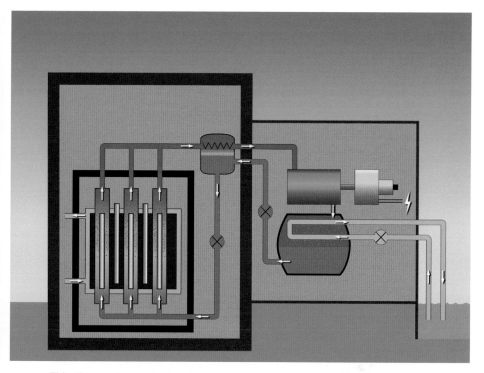

This diagram illustrates the workings of the reactor used in the Chernobyl power plant. The fuel rods (yellow) are surrounded by water that produce steam (red) when heated. The steam passes through a turbine, which drives the electricity generator. However, a flaw in the design increases power output when cooling water is lost.

Not only was it risky to disconnect this system, it was a violation of international safety laws. Grigori Medvedev, a former engineer who worked at the Chernobyl site for many years, wondered about Fomin's decision: "A person determined to make his mark as a leader, to distinguish himself in a prestigious sector and prove that a nuclear reactor . . . can function without cooling — such a person is capable of anything."

Shortly after 11:00 p.m. reactor #4's power level was dropped further, from 1600 MW to between 700 and 1000 MW—these are dangerously low levels. Another safety feature, local automatic control (LAC), which would have shut down the reactor if the power output dropped too low, was stopped. At very low output levels the fission process becomes highly unstable. When LAC sensors detect the output level dropping, the system either raises the output back up to a safe point (by increasing the amount of fission) or shuts down the reactor entirely. Anatoly Dyatlov, the deputy chief engineer who was overseeing the test, did not want the reactor shut down. He ordered that the LAC features be terminated. Dyatlov, like Fomin and Bryukhanov, had come to Chernobyl with no experience in nuclear technology.

At around 12:30 a.m. on April 26 the power output suddenly dropped to a critical 30 MW—far below safe levels. The fission process began producing a great deal of unwanted nuclides—variations of basic chemical elements, some of which are highly radioactive. When the nuclear fission process becomes poisoned with a high percentage of nuclides, it also becomes more difficult to control.

The operators at the control panel realized the only smart thing to do at that point was to shut the reactor down and reschedule the test for another time. However, Dyatlov ordered the output level to be raised so that the creation of the test conditions could continue. Dyatlov flew into a rage when two of the operators tried to defy these orders. Fearing for their jobs, the operators reluctantly gave in. Under impossible circumstances, they did their best—they were

Nuclides in More Detail

Nuclides are variations of the atoms of basic elements. The variation exists either in the number of protons, the number of neutrons, or the potential energy output. For example, normal uranium has 92 protons, but its electrons can vary from 141 (in the most common form of the element) to 146. Nuclides can be either stable (i.e., exhibit no radioactive decay) or unstable and emit radiation. Some elements have very few nuclides; others have many. While some exist in nature, others can only be produced in laboratories. Nuclides can be harmless to human life or they can be deadly. Nuclides in the latter group are unfortunately very commonly produced during the fission process.

As the reactor core became unstable, Chernobyl's control panel operators, such as those above, recommended that the test be stopped.

able to raise the output level back up to 200 MW by 1:00 a.m. Fission activity was still dangerously uneven, however, and nuclides continued to be produced by the millions.

At 1:03 a.m. six pumps were sending water into the reactor to keep it cool. Two additional pumps were then turned on. Having eight pumps delivering water to the reactor was another critical error; since the reactor's output had dropped, the extra water was not needed. As a result, not enough of the water became converted to steam, and the excess water began to drag down the reactor's power output even further.

The fission activity became more dangerous than ever. Furthermore, another safety feature—one that sensed when water levels inside the reactor were too high—was disabled. A similar safety feature that sensed when steam levels were too low had also been switched off.

At 1:22 a.m. one of the operators received a printout of the reactor's current condition. Output levels were far too low, the sluggish fission process was producing millions of nuclides, and the steam-to-water ratio in the reactor was far too low. The operators knew that the power plant's rules required the reactor to be shut down in these circumstances, but they feared reprisals from Dyatlov. In *Chernobyl: The Real Story*, Richard Mould noted that "the operator is required in the written rules to immediately shut down the reactor, since there is no automatic shutdown linked to this forbidden situation." At 1:23 a.m. the operators closed off the steam pipes that ran from the reactor core to turbogenerator #8. Because of this critical error, no steam was moving out of the core.

It is conceivable that the disaster could still have been averted had a final safety feature not been kept from functioning. When both turbogenerators stopped running, a trip switch—something like a circuit breaker—was supposed to turn off the reactor. Shutting it down was crucial because the steam inside it, having no place to go, would quickly raise the pressure in the reactor to a critical level. The trip switch, however, had been disabled. Ironically, the existence of the switch was never mentioned in the test plan that Bryukhanov sent for official approval, and so no one in authority would have known that there was a switch or that it had been disabled.

No Turning Back

With the clock still at 1:23 a.m., the overworked pumps feed-ing cooling water into the reactor began to have problems. The flow of cooling water dropped, and the water that was already there began to heat up. A deadly cycle began. The heating produced steam, the steam in turn encouraged yet more fission, and the fission produced more heat, which took the cycle back to its start. The operators at the control panels became alarmed. With all the steam channels to the turbo-generators blocked off, the reactor should not have been producing any steam, because the steam had no place to go.

The operators decided enough was enough. The lower-ranked of the two suggested that they engage the reactor's emergency power reduction system (EPRS), which was designed to shut down the reactor altogether by lowering a series of metal rods into the core. This was supposed to slow down the fission process until it stopped. The higher-ranked operator agreed with this plan and pressed the emergency button. What happened next was entirely unexpected. Because of a serious design flaw in the metal rods, the reac-tor did not shut down. The tips of the metal rods were made of graphite; graphite increases fission activity. Before the Chernobyl experiment, this increase in activity had never been noticed because under normal operating conditions, the increase in fission would have been relatively minor in comparison with the fission that was already taking place. Putting it another way, the reactor has no trouble absorbing this small jump in fission when it is operating normally.

However, the situation at that moment was anything but normal, and the surge in fission activity proved to be the last

Control rods, such as these, were inserted into the RBMK reactor to slow the fission activity taking place in the core. However, the rods increased the activity instead.

straw before disaster struck. The heat in the reactor rose to critical levels in a matter of seconds—far too quickly for any of the operators to respond—and the steam produced was far more than the reactor could hold. At around 1:24 a.m. the breaking point occurred—the channels that directed the steam outward (but were blocked from doing so) ruptured, and the superheated steam and water continued to push outward until the entire reactor container gave way. The result was a monstrous explosion.

Apocalyptic Destruction

The force of the explosion was such that the biological shield covering the reactor—a circular lid of solid concrete that weighed more than 1,000 tons (roughly 907,000 kg) and measuring almost 50 feet (15.2 meters) across—was blown off and became temporarily airborne. When it came back down, it landed at an angle. As Glenn Alan Cheney aptly put it, "The lid over the reactor, a thousand-ton concrete disk ten feet thick, flipped into the air like a nickel and came back down to rest in an almost vertical position." The reactor core—where fission was still taking place—was then exposed. The air that rushed into the cavity further stirred up the fission process and set off several more explosions. These explosions were of a chemical nature, likely fed by a mix of oxygen and hydrogen that had gathered in and around the damaged reactor.

The reactor's physical structure then blew apart, followed by the building around it. The roof was obliterated, and perhaps worst of all, the dangerous material that was previously contained within the reactor shot out in a fiery

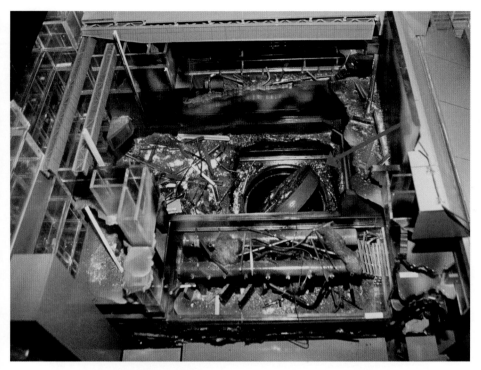

A model of the destroyed RBMK reactor core illustrates the 1,000 ton dislodged lid (center).

column—hunks of graphite, loads of nuclear fuel, and billions of radioactive particles. Much of the solid material was still flaming when it fell back to Earth, and some of it landed on the roof of the adjacent building, where turbogenerators #7 and #8 were housed. The roof of this building was coated with tar, and it quickly caught on fire. About 50 tons of nuclear fuel escaped into the atmosphere, and another 70, which were blown sideways, coated the damaged building and the grounds beyond.

The explosion at the Chernobyl nuclear power plant was so strong that it destroyed not only the reactor but the building around it as well.

One of the workers at the plant that night, an electrician named Iurii Badaev, remembered the moment:

> I was on shift forty metres from the reactor.
> We knew there were experiments going
> on. The experiments were according to a
> previously planned programme and we were
> following this programme. Our computer
> registers all deviations and records them
> on a special tape. We were watching over
> how the reactor was working. Everything
> was fine. Then a signal came which meant
> that the senior reactor engineer had pressed
> the button to switch the reactor totally off.
> Literally fifteen seconds later there was
> a sudden shock, and a few seconds later a
> stronger shock. The light went out and our
> machine cut out. But some sort of emergency
> [power] supply came on, and from that
> moment we tried to save the equipment,
> because everyone needs our information. . . .
> The machine was working and the diagnostic
> system was continuing. It was difficult to
> understand what it was registering. It was
> only then that we asked ourselves: what on
> earth has happened?

Another worker, a firefighter employed by the plant, remembered, "Suddenly I heard a strong burst of steam. We thought nothing of it, because steam was being let off practically all the time I was at work [it was a normal part of plant operations to release excess steam using what were called relief valves]. I was about to go and take a break, when there was an explosion. I rushed to the window. After the first explosion, there were others. I saw a black fireball which swirled up over the roof of the turbine hall, next to No. 4. unit."

While the harder material resulting from the explosions fell back to earth, the lighter-than-air material—specifically, the vast quantity of radioactive particles—remained

The remains of a burned-out turbine after the explosion.

in the skies over the ruined plant and was then picked up by the wind. Some of it fell back to earth in rain; some was carried away by the breezes. Winds were fairly strong at the time, and the radioactive dust began a deadly journey that soon proved the explosion was only the beginning of the nightmare.

Two

Causes of the Disaster

A CALAMITY OF THE SCALE of the Chernobyl disaster seldom has a single cause, whether it be faulty equipment or human error or anything else. Chernobyl was the result of a combination of elements, each of which has to be examined to understand how such a catastrophe could have occurred and to make sure it is not repeated in the future.

The Chernobyl Site

There were problems with the design of the Chernobyl site from the beginning—problems that were either never noticed or regarded as being relatively minor. A total of four reactors were built, each able to produce more than enough electricity for the surrounding towns and cities.

The Soviet government was proud of the new Chernobyl nuclear power plant. However, in their zeal to get the plant up and running as quickly as possible, the construction team was told to rush the building process. Consequently, walls and ceilings were mismeasured and crooked, cement ingredients were not proportioned or mixed correctly, and seals in containment areas were applied hastily and eventually

Cold War Competition

Aside from providing the region with electrical power, the Soviet government had another motive for building the Chernobyl power plant—its cold war competition with the United States. The term "cold war" refers to the almost fifty-year period following the end of World War II in 1945 during which diplomatic relations between the United States and the Soviet Union were tense, often perilously so. "Cold" referred to the fact that tensions never reached the "hot" point where the two powers openly warred with each other. Nonetheless, the two nations constantly tried to outdo each other in every way imaginable, including the control and exploitation of nuclear power.

became leaky. In addition, since many of the engineers involved in the construction had little or no experience with nuclear facilities, they were careless with the fine details.

Nonetheless, the first reactor was completed in 1977, followed by the other three in 1978, 1981, and 1983. During these years experts were already speaking out about the risks of shoddy reactor design. In their 1982 book *Nuclear Power: Both Sides*, Michio Kaku and Jennifer Trainer summarized the experts' concerns: "Many critics agree that a nuclear power plant operating in top form would probably be relatively safe. But they are convinced there is a wide gap between theory and practice; some reactors are poorly designed or constructed."

The Chernobyl Reactor

There are several different types of nuclear reactors. Model RBMK-1000 was the one used in the four Chernobyl systems and was designed along the same lines as those used in the Soviet Union's earliest reactors from the 1950s. RBMK is an acronym for the Russian words meaning "high-powered, chanel-type reactor." The design's antiquated and sometimes faulty features were already the subject of scrutiny in the 1980s. For example, many of the safety devices were too easily switched off or circumvented, allowing for conditions that were inherently unstable. Also, the RBMK reactors permitted fission levels to occasionally increase to dangerously high levels in the course of normal operation. When the water used as a coolant turned to gas (that is, water vapor), its ability to slow down the fission process was greatly reduced. In turn, fission output climbed rapidly. To compensate for

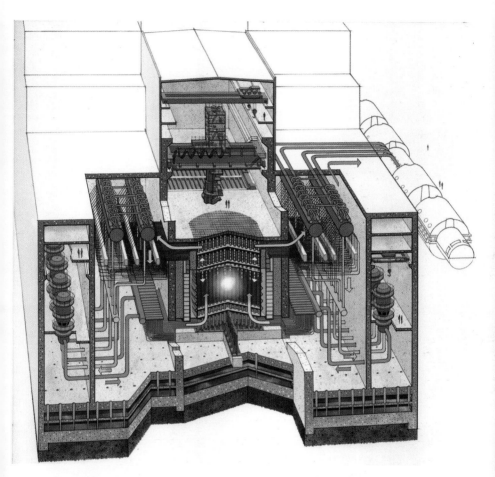

The RBMK-1000 reactor had been in use in Soviet nuclear power plants since the 1950s.

this failing, RBMK reactors had control rods that could be manually dipped into the core to absorb some of the fission products and thus slow down the reaction process. However, as noted in the previous chapter, on the RBMK, the

The Town of Pripyat

Pripyat was founded in 1970; it was built alongside the nuclear facility, with the intent that it be a convenient home for the plant's workers and their families. In time, Pripyat became a pleasant place to live, with schools, shops, parks and playgrounds, cottages, apartment blocks, churches, and all the other features of an ordinary municipality. When the nuclear plant became operational, hundreds and then thousands of people moved to Pripyat, hoping to build a future for themselves and their children. Although there were some initial concerns about living so close to a nuclear plant, the Soviet government dealt with them successfully.

tips of these rods were made of graphite, which momentarily increased fission rather than reduced it. Furthermore, the Chernobyl reactor had only thirty manual control rods—not enough to control the pending disaster in any case; it has since been determined as it should have had at least twice as many. All of these elements played a crucial role in the Chernobyl disaster.

The Soviet Public Relations Machine

The Soviet government was adept in the art of secrecy, particularly as it related to the distribution of information. Secrecy was a major factor in the Chernobyl disaster. Ordinary Soviet people had neither reliable information about nuclear power nor the right to influence decisions made about its use. Grigori Medvedev noted that the government's censorship of information was actually, "in essence, a huge barbed-wire barricade around the actions of the government and the [Communist] party."

Part of the Soviet public relations strategy for promoting nuclear power involved the publishing of articles by Soviet scientists. The scientists who wrote the articles, often at the prodding of the government, lavishly praised the idea of utilizing nuclear energy. One article stated, "It must be acknowledged that nuclear power has a brilliant future. Nuclear power has definite advantages over conventional energy. . . . Nuclear power stations hold great promise for the use of powerful reactors."

Most of these articles failed to mention the radioactive by-products of nuclear fission or other possible dangers. The Soviet government would not stand for dissent. Medvedev attempted to point out some of the weaknesses and, in his opinion, future problems of the Soviet nuclear industry in a series of articles written in the late 1970s. He had difficulty getting the articles published in the Soviet Union; indeed, he was warned against even trying. One editor, after reading the material, told him, "You know, it's powerful stuff. It's really a treacherous denunciation of the state in literary form. At a time of nuclear confrontation you have dared to lay bare the failings and negative aspects of our nuclear experience. They'll make mincemeat out of you. People have been hauled off to labor camps for much less."

A crucial aspect of the public relations campaign involved the selective disclosure of information pertaining to past nuclear-related incidents. In September 1957 some radioactive material escaped from a waste-storage tank in a facility in Chelyabinsk; several people were exposed, agricultural fields were contaminated, and livestock had to be destroyed. In May 1966, at a power station in the town of Melekess, two workers were irradiated after an unexpected power surge. In October 1975, at a plant in Leningrad, one of the reactor cores experienced a partial meltdown. None of this information or anything else of an adverse nature was made public.

It was even Soviet policy not to disclose such information to workers at other nuclear facilities. This irresponsibility played a key role in the downfall of the Chernobyl facility. According to Medvedev, "There was a conspiracy of silence. Mishaps were never publicized; and, as nobody knew about them, nobody could learn from them. For thirty-five years people did not notify each other about accidents at nuclear power stations, and nobody applied the experience of such accidents to their work. It was as if no accidents had taken place at all: everything was safe and reliable."

The Soviet Political System

During the 1980s the Soviet Union occupied a world of its own. It was controlled by people one never saw, it had laws in whose making one had no say, and it dispensed information one could not trust. Its governing system, communism, was based on the premise that all citizens were to work for the greater good. In practice, the bulk of what a person earned was taken by the government, which was entrusted to distribute the collective wealth evenly throughout the population. Medical care, clothing, food, and housing were free, and the government was the provider.

Communism, however, had countless problems. Perhaps the most obvious was its tendency to corrupt those who sought power within it. Ruthlessness in the pursuit of government positions was commonplace. Those in power who craved wealth readily found creative ways to redirect government funds to their own pockets. The most prominent people in Soviet society were those in the upper ranks of government, and the only way to get ahead was to please them.

What was true of government was equally true of the nuclear power industry. Nuclear power was a prestigious field, and those who worked in it were paid well. Almost as a consequence, men with very little expertise, few qualifications, and little training sought and all too often received desirable jobs. Many of them were required to make crucial decisions even though they knew little about the fine points of nuclear physics, and lower-ranking workers who better understood the dangers of nuclear power were scared to speak out. If there was a problem, it was often prudent to pretend that one did not notice it. These circumstances constituted a recipe for disaster.

Three

Cleanup and Cover-up

THE MEN IN THE CONTROL ROOM of reactor #4 tried to flow cooling water into the reactor in a desperate attempt to respond in some way to the crisis. However, the needles on the gauges lay on the zero point—an indication that the reactor did not exist anymore. Iurii Badaev, the plant worker quoted earlier, remembered his reaction:

> I rushed off along the usual route, but it was
> impossible to get to the [next] level. The
> elevator was crumpled, crushed tight shut,
> and there were blocks of reinforced concrete
> on the steps and some sort of tubs; but the
> main thing was that there was no light. We
> still didn't know the scale of the accident,
> nothing at all. Nonetheless, I wanted to
> get there and even ran off for a flashlight.
> And when I came back with the flashlight,
> I realized that I wouldn't get through. . . .
> Water was pouring from the ninth floor, it
> really was pouring.

Piers Paul Read stated that Dyatlov did not believe the reactor had been destroyed until he went outside.

> At his feet there were some smoldering lumps of . . . of what? They looked like graphite, but if they were graphite that could only mean. . . . It was dark. How could he tell? Perhaps they were lumps of concrete. He did not pause to inspect them but went back through a door to the control room of the third [reactor]. There the head of the shift asked him if he should shut down his reactor. Dyatlov said that it was unnecessary.

Radioactive particles were flying around everywhere. Individuals not wearing protective gear could absorb a lethal dose within minutes, perhaps even seconds. Almost nobody at the plant was wearing protective gear. Within an hour after the accident, many were already experiencing nausea and general weakness; in addition, their skin rapidly darkened—this condition is colloquially called a "nuclear tan." One engineer, after having been told to assess the extent of the damage, climbed onto the roof of a nearby building and looked down at the glow in the center of the reactor wreckage. In doing so, his body was assaulted with so much radioactivity that he died within weeks.

When the plant's director, Bryukhanov, finally realized the magnitude of what had happened, he made the decision to keep quiet about it, as he had been trained to do. W. Scott

Ingram noted, "Bryukhanov had followed the standard Soviet protocol for any accident. He did all in his power to reassure party leaders in Kiev and Moscow that the problem at Chernobyl was minor."

When firefighters began arriving on the scene to put out all the blazes, they were not told the details of what had happened. Many of them received lethal doses of radiation within minutes and became ill almost instantly. Of those who bravely fought the blazes, thirty-one died. One who survived told a harrowing story about the loss of several of his colleagues: "We didn't have much idea about radiation.

Candles are placed in front of a memorial dedicated to the firefighters who lost their lives as a result of the Chernobyl nuclear disaster.

Whoever was working didn't have any idea. The engines delivered the water . . . the water went up, and then those lads who died went up. . . . They scrambled up using a step-ladder. I helped them set it up, it was all done very quickly, all this was done, and I didn't see them again."

Leaving Their Homes Behind—Forever

Bryukhanov contacted political leaders in the nearby Ukrainian capital of Kiev and in Moscow and informed them he wanted to evacuate the town of Pripyat. He was told not to do so, as orders to evacuate might create a mass panic. There was also concern that word of the accident might spread. The Communist Party officials Bryukhanov spoke with initially did not understand the full extent of the damage, largely because of Bryukhanov's earlier, inaccurate assurances. They told him to do nothing until they saw what had happened for themselves.

The following day, April 27, both officials and scientists began arriving at the site and surveyed it without wearing any kind of protective gear. In the weeks and months ahead those people died horrible deaths. In the absence of an authoritative announcement about the true extent of the damage, the citizens of Pripyat continued with their daily lives as if nothing had happened.

Soviet officials finally agreed to evacuate the area after multiple instrument readings had convinced them of the alarmingly high levels of radiation. However, they still did not want the citizens to suspect the extremely serious nature of the disaster, even if it meant jeopardizing the

"Only Three Days"

The residents of Pripyat were instructed to bring along only the basic necessities they would need for three days and that they would be returning after that time. The implication was that the accident had not been that severe and that the evacuation was merely a precautionary measure. Assured that they would be returning in three days, the people remained calm, and the evacuation proceeded smoothly. One woman said, "They told us it would be for three days. Although they knew full well it would not be for three days, but for longer. I think it was quite proper that they said what they said. Otherwise, the evacuation would not have been carried out so quickly." Many of the people were smiling and joking as they boarded the buses, acting as though they were experiencing nothing more than a minor inconvenience. In truth, none of Pripyat's roughly 40,000 residents ever saw their homes again.

health of those managing the evacuation effort. Piers Paul Reid wrote, "From the point of view of the civil defense, the greatest danger was mass panic, leading to a disorganized exodus through possibly contaminated territory. For that reason, Berdov [one of the officials overseeing the evacuation] had ordered his men not to wear masks or respirators in the town; there were not enough for the whole population, and to distribute some to the few would cause panic among the many."

One woman whose husband had gone off to fight the fires at the plant recalled the scene on that first night following the decision to evacuate:

> One side of the street there are buses,
> hundreds of buses, they're already preparing
> the town for evacuation, and on the other
> side, hundreds of fire trucks. They came from
> all over. And the whole street is covered in
> white foam [a detergent used to wash away
> the radioactive particles]. We're walking on
> it, just cursing and crying. Over the radio
> they tell us they might evacuate the city
> for three or five days, take your warm
> clothes with you, you'll be living in the
> forest. In tents. People were even glad —
> a camping trip!

Another eyewitness from the town of Pripyat, a young mother, had the following horrid recollections:

A convoy of buses evacuates the residents of Pripyat after the accident.

All morning I had been doing the laundry
and hanging it out to dry on the balcony.
By evening it had already collected vast
amounts of radioactive dust. . . . Hardly
anyone among the builders and installers
knew anything. Then word came about an
accident and fire at No. 4 unit. But what
exactly happened, nobody knew. . . .

A group of children from our neighborhood bicycled over to the bridge near the Yanov station to get a good view of the damaged reactor unit. We later discovered that this was the most highly radioactive spot in town, as the radioactive cloud released during the explosion had passed right overhead. But none of this was known until later, and that morning, 26 April, the kids simply wanted to get a look at the burning reactor. They later came down with severe radiation sickness.

Pripyat was not the only community within range of the Chernobyl plant that had to be evacuated. There were some farming towns and villages in and around the outlying areas that had also become contaminated. Contacting the people in these regions proved challenging, as some properties were very large, and therefore the homes were far apart. Officials traveled from door to door and told the occupants they were required to leave their property at once—leave tracts of land that in many cases had been in a family for many generations. They, too, were not informed of the severity of the problem, most likely so that they would go along with the evacuation request without resistance.

Hiding the Truth—For a While

Soviet leaders did all in their power to keep the details of the accident from reaching the outside world. What little information they were willing to offer was designed to make

A satellite image taken a few days after the accident shows the spread of radioactive material (red) around the plant and its vicinity.

the incident seem relatively minor and the human suffering minimal. Zhores Medvedev wrote, "[It was] clear that the officials in Moscow did not understand that they were dealing with a catastrophe of global dimensions. There are signs, too, of an initial attempt to hide what had happened. . . . The decision-making process seems to have been deliberately slow to preserve a façade of 'business as usual.'"

The cover-up came to an end when other countries began to notice unusually high levels of radiation in their air. On Monday, April 28, workers at the nuclear plant in the small town of Forsmark, Sweden, became alarmed when radiation readings in the soil, in the air, on shrubs and trees, and from the bodies of their own employees suddenly rose to dangerous levels. Their first instinct was to think a problem had occurred at the Forsmark plant. After a round of tests, however, it was determined that all its reactors were operating normally. Soon technicians in the nearby nations of Denmark, Finland, and Norway were registering similar readings. With the help of weather reports that confirmed strong winds had been blowing recently across the Ukraine — including the Chernobyl area — it did not take long before the pieces of the puzzle came together.

By the time nuclear scientists in Sweden and other neighboring nations became aware of the radioactive fall-out, Mikhail Gorbachev, the Soviet president, knew his choices were limited. That same day, a statement was issued by the Soviet government that an accident had occurred at the Chernobyl power plant with one of the reactors and that they were working to clean it up and assist those who had been injured. No further details were offered, and the statement was released quietly in the hope that it would attract as little attention as possible.

Whatever the domestic effects of the Soviet statement, the full dangers of the accident were apparent to virtually

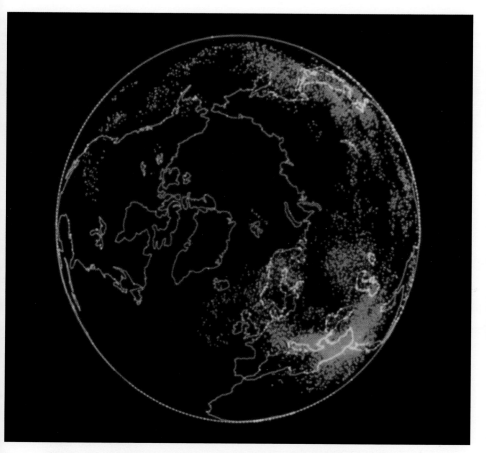

A computer simulation illustrates the distribution of radioactivity in the Northern Hemisphere ten days after the explosion at Chernobyl.

everyone in the developed world and served only to enrage many people. Travelers were warned to stay away from potentially affected areas, and some nations, especially those in central and southern Europe, lost millions of dollars in tourist-related revenue. Millions of dollars more were lost when radioactive material contaminated the farming regions

Mikhail Gorbachev

The highest official in the Soviet Union at the time of the accident was the country's president, Mikhail Gorbachev. At fifty-four years of age, he was the youngest man to lead the Communist Party in decades. When he first took power, many feared he would continue his government's secretive and often underhanded policies. Practical and realistic by nature, however, Gorbachev began making radical changes in political policy and practice.

One particularly striking change came to be known as glasnost, a Russian word that means "openness" or "publicity." This openness involved the Soviet Union's becoming more forthcoming with the rest of the world concerning its own inner workings. The first big test of glasnost was the Chernobyl accident. Gorbachev had to decide how much information to authorize the Soviet government to reveal to the world. He was in a very difficult position, as he wanted to stay faithful to the glasnost idea but also protect the reputation of his country. He began cautiously, giving out only the most basic details. As further information leaked out on its own, and other nations demanded greater transparency, however, Gorbachev was forced to provide a more detailed account of the accident. Nevertheless, many believe certain facts were never revealed and that the full truth will never be known.

of the European and Asian nations closest to Chernobyl. People lined up by the thousands to be tested for exposure. Many had to stay indoors until their areas could be cleared of radioactive dust. The damage caused by the Soviets' refusal to report the accident immediately after it occurred is impossible to fully estimate.

Reaction Around the World

As more facts became available, dismay and outrage were expressed all around the world and by every stratum of society—by the media, by political leadership, and by ordinary citizens. The U.S. secretary of state, George Shultz, made the following terse statement: "When an incident has cross-border implications, there's an obligation under international law to inform others and to do it promptly. We don't think [the Soviets] provided what they should have." Just days later President Ronald Reagan made a similar statement: "The Soviets owe the world an explanation. A full accounting of what happened at Chernobyl and what is happening now is the least the world community has a right to expect." An article that appeared in *Time* magazine a few weeks after the accident reported outrage by several European leaders:

> [They] were furious with the Soviets for
> initially concealing the disaster, and fearful
> of its health effects. Said Swedish Energy
> Minister Birgitta Dahl, "We shall reiterate
> our demand that the whole Soviet civilian
> nuclear program be subject to international
> control." In West Germany, Foreign Minister

Four British newspapers announce the Chernobyl nuclear accident.

Hans-Dietrich Genscher urged Moscow
to shut all nuclear power plants similar to
the one at Chernobyl. The West Germans
asked that an international team be allowed
to visit the site. Danish Prime Minister Poul
Schluter called the situation "intolerable and
extremely worrying."

U.S. president Ronald Reagan believed that the Soviets owed the world an explanation and a full account of the accident at Chernobyl.

Ordinary citizens were also invited to give their opinions. In Poland one irate Warsaw resident was quoted as saying, "We can understand an accident. It could happen to anyone. But that the Soviets said nothing and let our children suffer exposure to this cloud for days is unforgivable."

Despite the widespread outrage, all was not doom and gloom on the international front. In Japan, for example, one Tokyo resident commented, "There is no sense of a growing crisis here. Not a single friend of mine is worried about radiation." In Scotland a water researcher said, "We take water from lochs and streams and reservoirs as well as springs, but we are watching the levels carefully and think there is no need for concern." After the initial panic and fervor died down, leaders of the seven major industrialized nations issued a joint statement: "We have discussed the implications of the accident at the Chernobyl nuclear power station. We express our deep sympathy to those affected. We remain ready to extend assistance, in particular medical and technical, as and when requested." Farther along in this statement was a noteworthy declaration: "Nuclear power is and, properly managed, will continue to be an increasingly widely used source of energy."

Cleanup Efforts: A Deadly Affair

The cleanup effort at the Chernobyl plant went on for many days. The first priority was to put all the fires out. There were flames not only within the exposed reactor core but also on the surrounding buildings and nearby grounds. There were several different ways to extinguish them. Those blazes that were too hot to be doused by water were smothered with sand. Many of the firefighters doing this work were exposed to more radiation in a half hour than ordinary people absorb in a lifetime, and they began to show symptoms almost immediately. One later recalled, "Alexsandr Petrovskii and I went up onto the roof of the machine room; on the way we met the kids from Specialized Military Fire Brigade No. 6; they were in a bad way. . . . After finishing the job we went back down, where the ambulance picked us up. We, too, were in a bad way."

The fire in the reactor core was particularly difficult to quell, as it was burning at temperatures exceeding 4000 degrees Fahrenheit (2204.4 degrees Celsius). Helicopters began covering it with sand, as well as lead, clay, dolomite, and boron, first in small bags packed by volunteers and then in parachutes that had been turned upside down and loaded with as much weight as the helicopters could carry.

It was not until May 6 that all the blazes were finally out and the debris cleanup could begin. This dangerous undertaking was performed by people who became known

Liquidators clean radioactive debris from the roof of reactor 3.

as the Chernobyl liquidators. These workers were not told the full extent of the radiation danger in the area, but they were promised good pay, extra rations of food and alcohol, and in some cases early retirement complemented by a sizable pension. Otherwise healthy individuals were given only minimal protective gear—sometimes nothing more than cotton surgical masks and rubber gloves—and instructed to work in contaminated areas for no more than a few minutes at a time.

In some areas the cleanup crews were exposed to more than 10,000 times the allowable dose of radiation. They shoveled pieces of shattered graphite and still-smoldering chunks of nuclear fuel into the glowing crater, never realizing they were signing their own death warrants. Others, working farther away from the plant, washed radioactive dust from homes and other buildings, dug up contaminated layers of topsoil from farmlands, buried thousands of movable items (even as large as cars and trucks) in underground concrete vaults, and cut down trees and shrubs, since they were capable of absorbing and storing high levels of radioactive material that could be rereleased into the atmosphere in the event of a fire. It was a grim experience, as one liquidator later remembered:

> We were between twenty-five and forty
> [years old], some of us had university
> degrees, or vocational-technical degrees.
> For example, I am a history teacher. Instead
> of machine guns they gave us shovels. We
> buried trash heaps and gardens. The women

A worker in protective garments piles contaminated vegetables into a landfill in Germany, May 1986.

in the villages watched us and crossed
themselves. We had gloves, respirators, and
surgical robes. The sun beat down on us.
We showed up in their yards like demons.
They didn't understand why we had to
bury their gardens, rip up their garlic and

cabbage when it looked like ordinary garlic and ordinary cabbage. The old women would cross themselves and say, "Boys, what is this—is it the end of the world?"

Another Explosion?

Not long after the Chernobyl incident, scientists at the scene came to a grim realization—another explosion could occur at any time. It would happen if the still-burning nuclear fuel sitting in the reactor crater, along with thousands of pounds of other glowing debris, burned its way through the reactor floor. Underneath the reactor was a bubbler pool filled with thousands of gallons of water. If the nuclear fuel and other burning wastes were to make contact with all this water, it would trigger another steam explosion.

The only way to avoid this possibility was to get inside the pool and open the sluice gates to release the water. Three men agreed to undertake this dangerous task. In spite of wearing diving suits for protection, none of the three ever came out alive—the radioactive material that contaminated the water had turned it into a corrosive acid. Before they died, the men managed to open the sluice gates, and the radioactive water was able to be pumped out of the basement.

Hospital Overload

In the weeks and months following the accident, hospitals in and around the region became inundated with patients suffering from radiation poisoning. Since this was a situation unlike any other, many health care professionals had no idea how to respond. At the Pripyat Medical Center, for example, which began receiving the first patients immediately after the accident, the staff did not have the necessary equipment to accurately diagnose the conditions of the patients they were receiving. Many of the nurses and doctors on duty had little or no experience with radiation exposure.

Intuition and common sense at least told medical providers there and elsewhere to keep the Chernobyl patients away from those with normal ailments. Doctors and nurses approached the affected patients wearing gloves and masks and tried their best to minimize direct contact even during treatment. Many received ordinary showers in an attempt to cleanse them of radioactive particles. The showers usually had no effect, however, since most of the dangerous nuclides had been absorbed into the patients' skin by then and had begun their destructive course. All radiation patients were kept together in isolated areas; this was another costly mistake since those with less exposure to radioactive material were put in close quarters with those who were still contagious from much greater exposure.

The physical symptoms of prolonged exposure to high levels of radiation include fever, muscle and joint pain, shortness of breath and other breathing difficulties, a metallic taste in the mouth, blurred vision, dizziness, nausea, vomiting, and diarrhea. As the condition progresses, the symptoms worsen: the skin darkens (and, in cases with radiation burns, lesions with a crispy texture form); portions of skin rip open easily and can hang from the body like torn cloth; blistering, extreme swelling, open sores, and loosening of muscle tissue from bone become widespread; and internal organs and other tissues break down and eventually disintegrate.

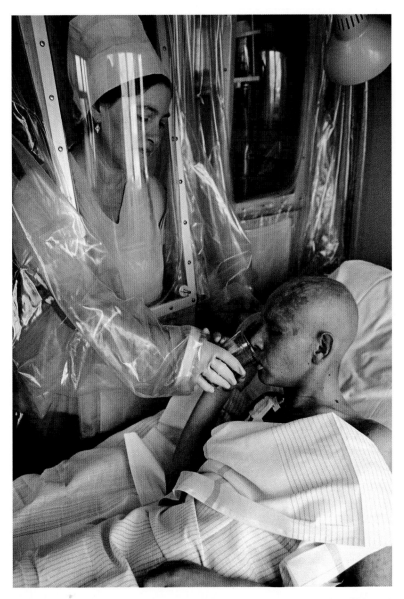

A Chernobyl survivor is treated for radiation exposure and burns in a Moscow hospital.

The Sarcophagus

In early May, after the fires had been doused and the major cleanup project started, one ongoing problem became clear to nuclear experts—the exposed core of the former reactor would continue to produce dangerously radioactive nuclides for years to come. There was simply no way of turning off this process; the only hope was to contain it somehow. The eventual solution was the construction of a concrete and steel enclosure around the damaged site—an enclosure that would take on the macabre name the Sarcophagus. Once completed, the enclosure would isolate the wrecked reactor from the immediate environment and thus reduce the local level of radioactivity and enable workers to continue operating the other three reactors on the Chernobyl site. It was particularly important to continue operating the other reactors because many of the surrounding communities that had not been overly affected by the accident still relied on the Chernobyl plant for electricity.

The slow construction process began as soon as the massive cleanup project around the site was finished. Miles of steel were used to erect the skeletal structure; next thousands of tons of concrete were poured into huge individual blocks created far from the site so as not to contaminate the workers. The blocks were then driven to the site and set into place one at a time with the help of several cranes. Progress was slowed by the fact that the workers could not remain on the site for long periods.

When it was finally completed in December 1986, the Sarcophagus stood nearly thirty stories high. Radiation levels

The Sarcophagus, a concrete and steel structure, covers the damaged
reactor at Chernobyl.

did, in fact, drop far enough for the other three reactors to begin normal operations again. In light of this successful outcome, many officials in the Soviet government considered the Chernobyl nightmare to be over. In some ways, however, it was only beginning.

Four
Lingering Dark

IN THE YEARS FOLLOWING THE CHERNOBYL accident, the Soviet government found itself in a precarious position as it scrambled to minimize the public relations damage. It also had to address the consequences of the disaster, consequences it was trying vigorously to hide. When Grigori Medvedev was working on his book *The Truth about Chernobyl*, he interviewed one nuclear worker who got into trouble with the Soviet government simply for speaking to him. The worker later recalled a government intelligence agent saying angrily, "I'm asking why you have been giving Medvedev information about Chernobyl. You work in the nuclear section, where you hear things and you know things. You know all that precisely because you work here. This is the central government apparatus, and such information must not be divulged to anyone. You are engaged in important, almost secret work. Chernobyl is a state secret."

The Zone of Exclusion
Not long after the Chernobyl accident, scientists and government officials declared the immediate area around the

site off-limits to all but the most critical personnel. This area of high contamination, which became known as the zone of exclusion, was at first designed as a space enclosed by four concentric circles, the innermost portion (the area immediately around the reactor site) being the most dangerous and the outermost portion the least dangerous.

Over the years, however, as scientists became better able to determine the specific areas that were most radioactive, the mapping of contamination was adjusted. Unsurprisingly, many of the hottest, or most radioactive, sectors were those closest to the Chernobyl power plant. However, there were also several to the northeast, in eastern Belarus and in southwestern Russia. These areas became contaminated when wind and rain carried billions of radioactive particles through the air in the days following the accident. Some of the spread was even caused by those trying to fight it. One observer wrote, "The lead that helicopters dropped into the flaming crater evaporated and blew across the countryside. It finds its way into people via grass that cows eat. It is impossible to say how much of this lead is from gasoline, how much from Chernobyl, but whatever the source, it's all over the place."

The immediate zone of exclusion around the Chernobyl power plant measures 18.6 miles (30 km). It has also been called the zone of alienation, Chernobyl zone, fourth zone, and simply the Zone.

Ongoing Health Problems

The greatest cost of the Chernobyl disaster was the human cost. In the years immediately following the accident, health

An officer stands guard at the checkpoint of the Chernobyl nuclear power plant's exclusion zone in Kozhushi, a village in the Republic of Belarus.

problems in many contaminated areas began to rise, some dramatically. The greatest difficulty in gathering concrete statistics lay in the fact that it was not possible to track down every case related to the accident and also to reliably link each one directly to radiation exposure. It is important to

A Strange Opportunity for Rebirth

In the years following the accident, the Zone of Exclusion has become home to a variety of wildlife, both plants and animals, that were either dropping in number when humans lived there or had disappeared entirely. Animals from the lynx to the boar to the eagle owl—none of which had occupied the area around the Chernobyl plant for decades—have experienced a kind of localized rebirth. Even bears, which have not be in the region for centuries, have staged a modest reemergence. Perhaps the most striking example of this phenomenon is the numerous bird species that are not only thriving but have been seen nesting—and producing viable eggs—around the steel and concrete enclosure that was erected around the site of Reactor # 4, perhaps the most irradiated and dangerous area with the Zone.

It wasn't always like this. In the weeks and months immediately following the disaster, wildlife suffered just as people did. Most either died or, at the very least, were no longer able to reproduce. Even the plants and trees were affected—many went brown and died, earning the region the nickname "the Red Forest." Then, unexpectedly, it all began to come back, converting Pripyat into a bizarre society of man-made structures and animal residents. And while there have been reports of plant and animals experiencing mutations due to the increased radiation levels, it does not appear that this has occurred with any consistency—certainly not to the degree many scientists expected.

Ukrainian officials know certain precautions still need to be taken. The animals that live in the Zone of Exclusion, for example, cannot be used for food. And the flora also poses certain dangers—the government has spent time and money to keep the trees, shrubs, and other plant life to a minimum due to the risk of fire, which would release the radioactive particles they contain back into the air.

note that the global medical profession did not have any experience dealing with cases of this nature at the time, as such a tragedy had never occurred before. With no previous nuclear accidents on this scale to study, there were no case histories upon which to base diagnoses or treatments.

Despite the absence of precedents, it is clear that the radioactive fallout from the Chernobyl explosions stirred to life a collection of maladies that brought widespread suffering and death. The information that health care providers have been able to gather is undeniable. A variety of cancers have occurred with a marked increase in frequency since April 1986, including leukemia, breast cancer in women, lung and stomach cancer in men, and thyroid cancer in children.

Cancer is by no means the only lingering illness spawned by Chernobyl's fallout. Cases of respiratory ailments such as asthma and pneumonia have risen sharply, as have cardiovascular problems, including heart attacks, many of them fatal and occurring in relatively young patients. Radiation is known to have a weakening effect on muscle tissue, and the human heart is largely musculature. Thinning of the blood, another health problem that has become more common, can lead to various forms of hemorrhaging.

Birth defects and miscarriages have also become frequent; many women, fearing the possible risks to a fetus as well as to themselves, are choosing not to have children. As a result, the death rate in Ukraine is now greater than the birthrate. Linda Walker, the author of *Living after Chernobyl: Ira's Story*, tells the following about Ira, the young girl who serves as the focus of the book:

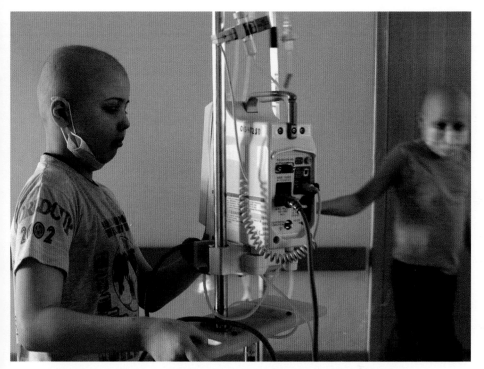

Both these children from Belarus have been diagnosed with lymphoma.
Winds carrying the heaviest radioactive material from the Chernobyl disaster
traveled across that republic.

[She] was born just two years after the
Chernobyl disaster, in a village called
Tihinichi, in the north of the Gomel Region.
Gomel is the most contaminated part of
Belarus, and there has been an estimated
80 percent rise in the number of children
born with disabilities in this area since the
Chernobyl accident. Ira was born with

Iodine 131: The Most Likely Culprit in Thyroid Cases

One of the many nuclides that spewed out from the Chernobyl explosions was a form of the element iodine called iodine 131(^{131}I). It is known to have a destructive effect on the thyroid, particularly in children, where it greatly increases the chance of cancer development.

The thyroid is a gland located in the neck that bears the shape of a butterfly with its wings spread. It plays a role in the body's use of energy, the creation of certain proteins, and the way the body reacts to other hormones.

Iodine has many useful medical applications, including purifying water, cleaning topical wounds, sterilizing the skin for surgery, reducing bacterial conjunctivitis, and treating eye infections. The body needs to ingest a certain amount of iodine to remain healthy, which it does through the diet. In fact, too little iodine will result in an iodine deficiency, which can lead to symptoms such as anemia, drowsiness, puffiness in the hands and face, mental apathy, and slowed or slurred speech.

The problem with the ^{131}I isotope is that the thyroid gland cannot distinguish it from the regular, stable forms of iodine, nor does it have a mechanism for rejecting this form. This isotope is radioactive and damages the thyroid as it decays. For those who have been exposed to ^{131}I, either in the air or through their diet (e.g., when ^{131}I particles have settled on their food prior to consumption), tablets with ordinary iodine can be taken as a preventive measure. However, there was only a very limited amount available to Pripyat residents immediately following the Chernobyl disaster.

Before to the accident, only two cases of thyroid cancer were diagnosed in the Ukraine in 1986. Now, according to the World Health Organization, the number of people who were children at the time of the accident and will develop thyroid tumors could reach as high as 50,000. This is to say nothing of affected children in Russia, Belarus, and elsewhere.

damage to all her limbs: Her legs are
very short and her feet twisted inward;
her arms are also short, and her left
hand twists outward. Her disabilities
were very likely caused by her mother's
exposure to radiation.

There are also indications that people's immune systems
have become diminished since the accident. Many doctors
have reported a startling increase in the number of common
health problems, including allergies, stomachaches, head-
aches, and colds. This particular phenomenon is sometimes
called Chernobyl AIDS. As one researcher noted, "What
they're dealing with is a syndrome resulting from a massive
attack on the body's immune system. The [nuclides] make
themselves right at home, radiating the immediately surrounding areas and all the blood that passes by. Put it all
together and it spells AIDS."

It is interesting to note that the Soviet president, Mikhail
Gorbachev, made the following statements during a television address just a few weeks after the accident: "I have
every reason to say that, despite the utter gravity of what
happened, the damage has turned out to be limited. . . .
Thanks to the effective measures taken, it is possible to say
today that the worst is past. The most serious consequences
have been averted."

Wastelands

In spite of the promises from Soviet officials that residents of
Pripyat would be able to return to their homes in three days,

virtually none did. In fact, the town was soon surrounded by fencing to keep them out. The land surrounding the Chernobyl plant became unusable, the plants, soil, and water too contaminated. One scientist who initially thought the farmlands might still be useful wrote just a few months after the accident, "Chernobyl soils are quite suitable for seeding perennial cereal grasses. . . . The fact is that radionuclides have virtually no effect on them . . . the land will return to normal, full-blooded life." The land never did return to its previous state.

The damage extended well beyond the Ukraine, Belarus, and Russia, reaching agricultural communities in parts of northern and eastern Europe as well. Staple crops in several European nations—which were critical not just to the farmers who grew them but to the consumers—had to be prematurely cut down, and the land remained unused until several inches of topsoil could be replaced. Dairy-based products such as milk, butter, chocolate, and ice cream were banned because they came from cows that had eaten contaminated grasses. Some of the animals were unable to give birth because of the radiation's effect on their reproductive systems. Many adult animals were euthanized and their bodies destroyed because they were no longer suitable for human consumption. Other nations refused to take agricultural products from these places for a few years. The loss to the European farm industry amounted to more than $300 million in the late 1980s—a figure that in terms of the 2010 dollar would be substantially higher.

Those who were evacuated from the most severely contaminated areas eventually resigned themselves to the fact

A German farmer plows over his spinach crop after its contamination by Chernobyl's radioactive fallout.

that they would never be able to return. In the mid–1990s the Ukrainian government determined that a full 5 percent of their nation was still unsuitable for human habitation—a total of more than 13,500 square miles (34,965 km²).

On Trial

Under intense pressure from the rest of the world and from President Gorbachev, who sought to continue his policy of greater transparency, Soviet officials convened a formal trial concerning the Chernobyl disaster in July 1987. It was held in the mostly empty town of Chernobyl itself; many felt it would be appropriate to get as close to the disaster zone as health considerations would permit. Bryukhanov, Fomin, and Dyatlov had been arrested shortly after the accident. Bryukhanov and Dyatlov kept their wits about them in the weeks and months that followed, seemingly in acceptance of their fate, but Fomin went through periods of near insanity and even tried to commit suicide. Three other plant employees were charged as well—Alexander Kovalenko, one of reactor #4's supervisors, Boris Rogozhkin, who oversaw the night shift, and Yuri Laushkin, a government safety inspector for the Chernobyl power plant. It was Bryukhanov, Fomin, and Dyatlov, however, who drew the most attention and criticism for their role in the tragedy. Prior to the trial, more than sixty-five other workers at the Chernobyl plant were either fired or demoted, and nearly half were stripped of their Communist Party membership altogether—a devastating blow to one's social status in itself.

The trial began on July 7 and, in spite of the Soviet government's promises of glasnost, journalists from around the world were permitted to watch only the first session and the final session. Bryukhanov was willing to accept partial blame, although he refused to admit to any personal violation of safety rules. Dyatlov stubbornly insisted he was not directly responsible for anyone's death, although he did

Plant director Viktor Bryukhanov (left), deputy chief engineer Anatoly Dyatlov (center), and chief engineer Nikolai Fomin (right) stand trial in July 1987 for the disaster at Chernobyl.

finally admit, "With so many human deaths, I cannot say I am completely innocent."

The trial ended with all six men being found guilty. The judge, Raimond Brize, spoke of the lackadaisical attitudes of supervisors around the Chernobyl plant; he said they created an "atmosphere of lack of control and lack of responsibility at the station. . . . People played cards and dominoes and wrote letters while they were on shift." He also determined that more than seventy violations of safety regulations had been committed in the years prior to the accident, many of which were covered up by plant administrators. Then he handed down his verdict—Bryukhanov, Fomin, and Dyatlov each received sentences of ten years' imprisonment in a labor camp. None served the full term.

Five

Legacy

WITH MORE THAN TWENTY YEARS of hindsight, what has humankind learned from the harrowing legacy of the Chernobyl power plant disaster? What lessons can be culled from the pain and suffering? What has changed for the better and what has not?

Getting Better

The RBMK-1000 reactor design that played a critical role in the disaster has been abandoned. Since April 1986 no new reactors were completed following this blueprint, and the few RBMK reactors that continue to operate have been retrofitted with features that make them safer. Many others have since been decommissioned altogether, and pressure has been brought to bear on those that are still being used, even with the improvements.

The Soviet system that was so firmly entrenched at the time of the accident—and in some ways played a part in it—is no more. By the end of 1991, the Soviet Union was formally dissolved, and the fifteen republics formerly under Soviet rule established themselves as free and independent nations. One of those fifteen was Ukraine.

Finding the Facts

While Ukrainians may have appreciated their newfound autonomy, they also had the ongoing Chernobyl issue to deal with. Many affected by the disaster who were still alive and reasonably healthy demanded increased health benefits and financial remuneration, as well as simple answers.

Officials from the former Soviet Union either had few answers to give, or they outright refused to deliver them. Some even accused supposedly objective agencies of playing a role in the subterfuge. In 2006 one journalist wrote, "United Nations nuclear and health watchdogs have ignored evidence of deaths, cancers, mutations and other conditions after the Chernobyl accident." He went on to write that a group of leading scientists and physicians believe that "at least 30,000 people are expected to die of cancers linked directly to severe radiation exposure in 1986 and up to 500,000 people may have already died." The article went on to say that the International Atomic Energy Agency and World Health Organization stood firm in their belief that only fifty deaths resulted from the disaster and that no more than four thousand people would eventually die from the Chernobyl accident.

The credibility of the World Health Organization is beyond any doubt, but it is also difficult to pinpoint exact figures when so much information is kept under wraps. Statistics on cancer rates in contaminated areas are notoriously unreliable, owing to government meddling. In subsequent years, when cancers began to appear in patients living within the range of Chernobyl contamination, many physicians were either instructed not to connect the cancers with radiation exposure or to adjust statistics to suggest that fewer people were exposed to radiation than really were. Many of the hundreds of thousands of liquidators who worked to clean up the site were moved by the Soviet government to places around the nation, where they would no longer be able to speak with their colleagues. Lists of those who had died or became seriously ill as a result of the cleanup effort have been conveniently lost or have mysteriously disappeared.

Is It Time to Go Nuclear?

The debate over the use of nuclear energy to produce electricity rages on. Those who support the nuclear option point out that it can provide an essentially unlimited supply of energy (because the odds of running out of appropriate atoms required for fission is fairly slim) and that nuclear energy is cleaner than fossil-fuel energy, that is, it produces less carbon pollution. In addition, some Americans and others who worry about the extent of their countries' dependence on imported oil, coal, and other fuels have noted that wider use of nuclear energy would markedly reduce the need for importation of these products. For these proponents, utilization of nuclear energy is linked to national security concerns. Also, the industry's supporters argue that accidents involving nuclear energy, while always regrettable and potentially terrible, are a normal, albeit unfortunate, aspect of scientific progress. There has been, they say, no scientific advancement that did not come without some cost.

Some of those who advocate wider use of nuclear energy consider the debate largely academic. They see nuclear power as part of the future, whether or not anyone likes it. As one author wrote, "Because all sources of energy based on fire are limited and non-renewable (or are renewed too slowly to keep pace with humankind's needs), most scientists have linked further progress to nuclear energy."

Setting aside the inherent dangers for a moment, the value of nuclear energy is hard to deny in a world where forms of clean energy have become so important. An article in the *Washington Post* from November 2009 tells an interesting story in this respect.

> When a brigade of Greenpeace activists stormed a nuclear power plant on the shores of the North Sea a few years ago, scrawling "danger" on its reactor, [Stephen] Tindale was their commander. Then head of the group's British office, he remembers, he stood outside the plant just east of London telling TV crews all the reasons "why nuclear power was evil." The construction of nuclear plants was banned in Britain for years after the 1986 Chernobyl disaster in what was then the Soviet Union. But now the British are weighing the idea of new nuclear plants as part of the battle against climate change, and Tindale is among several environmentalists who are backing the plan. "It really is a question about the greater evil—nuclear waste or climate change," Tindale said. "But there is no contest anymore. Climate change is the bigger threat, and nuclear is part of the answer."

The article continues, "Experts also point to a host of improvements in nuclear technology since the Chernobyl accident and the partial meltdown of the Three Mile Island plant in Pennsylvania in 1979. Most notable is an 80 percent drop in industrial accidents at the world's 436 nuclear plants since the late 1980s, according to the World Association of Nuclear Operators."

Many still oppose nuclear power and would like to see it altogether abandoned. While it is true that there have been no major nuclear-related incidents since Chernobyl, the truth is there have been many minor occurrences that could have led to a second Chernobyl but did not, sometimes through sheer luck. A 2007 report prepared for the European Parliament (the primary legislative body of the European Union) titled "Residual Risk: An Account of Events in Nuclear Power Plants since the Chernobyl Accident in 1986" states, "Every year there are thousands of incidents, occurrences and events in nuclear installations and, simply because there was no catastrophic radioactive leakage, the world reacts as if there was no problem." The report goes on to detail chilling examples of nuclear near-catastrophes and their causes, including reactor construction flaws, equipment failures, containment leakages, human error, violation of safety rules, and much more.

The problems and failings listed above suggest that human control of the atom is limited at best. It is important to keep this consideration in mind when taking note of the fact, for example, that nearly 20 percent of the electricity produced in the United States alone is generated by nuclear power.

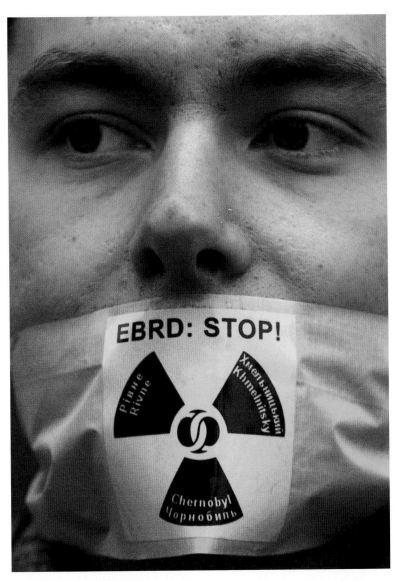

An activist from the National Ecological Centre of Ukraine participates in an anti-nuclear energy protest in Kiev.

In Belgium that number is more than 50 percent, and in France it is more than 75 percent. Until advances are made in capturing the energy provided by the sun, wind, and water, the debate as to whether there really is a need to keep taking these risks is likely to continue. Until that day comes, there will certainly be people who assert that nuclear power is in fact as close to a perfect form of energy as there is ever likely to be. For them the central question becomes: Should what could be a truly beneficial form of energy be abandoned because of the nuclear disaster in Chernobyl (and other, smaller accidents elsewhere)?

The Scene of the Crime Today

In the meantime, what of the formerly beautiful city of Pripyat and the looming presence of the Chernobyl nuclear facility responsible for its ruin? The city is still a ghost town, unsuitable for daily human life. Many experts believe it will remain so for centuries. Many of the former residents' possessions are still sitting in their homes and in the buildings they left in 1986 after being told they would return in a few days.

As for the Chernobyl power plant, the other three reactors continued to operate after the accident to supply the pressing electrical needs of local residents. When a fire broke out in one of reactor #2's turbines in 1991, the damage was extensive enough that officials decided to shut down the reactor for good rather than make repairs. Subsequently, nuclear scientists and concerned political leaders around the world urged the Ukrainian government to close the Chernobyl plant once and for all. The government finally capitulated and terminated reactor #1 in 1996 and reactor #3 in December 2000.

Abandoned apartment buildings loom over the city of Pripyat, once home to 50,000 people.

The site still employs hundreds of people, mostly for the purpose of monitoring the safety of the remaining equipment as well as the stockpiles of spent nuclear fuel. This fuel is housed in containment areas that are not built for long-term use, and thus projects are underway to build more durable enclosures and then move the spent fuel into them. Inside the damaged reactor, fission continues unabated. Some experts believe the area will not be safe for thousands of years. Even around the ruins of reactor #4, there will likely be no significant progress for perhaps three hundred years or more.

The Chernobyl power plant currently employs people who monitor the power station and its spent fuel.

As for the Sarcophagus, there are already known leaks and other structural problems. In 2007 plans were announced to design a new structure, called the New Safe Confinement, large enough to cover the Sarcophagus, arrest the further leakage of nuclides, and house unspent quantities of nuclear fuel for at least a hundred years. It is believed the project will cost well over $1 billion and not be completed until 2012. There is some irony in the fact that humans will likely have to build yet another containment facility in the next century—and perhaps in each of the centuries after that, for thousands of years to come.

The Human Element

Perhaps the greatest mistakes made during the Chernobyl disaster were human—the carelessness, the flawed design work, the cover-ups and other governmental corruption, and so on. Many blame nuclear energy and the awesome power of the atom, but maybe a more penetrating look at human nature will uncover the real cause. If those responsible had acted in a more mature, professional, and sensible manner, would the disaster have occurred in the first place? There is no doubt that nuclear energy is a tremendous force, one that needs to be handled with great care and caution. The need for care and caution, however, is not confined to the quest for a greater understanding of the technology. The specifically human contribution to the Chernobyl disaster and other, less egregious nuclear mishaps suggests a better understanding of human nature is also highly desirable.

As the father of one young victim put it, "I want to bear witness: my daughter died from Chernobyl. And they want us to forget about it."

Timeline

1917   The British chemist and physicist Ernest Rutherford splits the atom.

1932   The British physicist James Chadwick discovers the neutron.

1938   A team of European scientists conducts the first fission experiments with uranium.

1942   The world's first operational nuclear reactor is built at the University of Chicago.

1945   On August 6, an atomic bomb is dropped on the city of Hiroshima, Japan; a second is dropped on the city of Nagasaki three days later.

1948   The U.S. government, along with the Westinghouse Corporation, announces plans to utilize nuclear power for the creation of publicly consumed electricity.

1952   The first major nuclear plant accident occurs at the Chalk River facility in Ontario, Canada. Several mechanical failures combined with a series of operator errors led to hydrogen explosions that damaged the reactor core. As a result, fission by-products escaped through the reactor stacks and into the atmosphere.

1954   The Soviet Union builds the first nuclear reactor that produces enough electricity to power a community's electricity grid.

1955   In the United States, Arco, Idaho, becomes the first town to receive all of its electricity from nuclear power.

1970 In what is now Ukraine, construction begins on the Chernobyl nuclear power plant, along with the city of Pripyat to house the plant's workers.

1979 The nuclear plant at Three Mile Island, near Pennsylvania's capital, Harrisburg, suffers a core meltdown after the malfuction of a water pump, followed by a relief valve's failure to close. As a result, a variety of radioactive gases — including a small quantity of iodine 131 — is released into the atmosphere. Although future investigations of the incident will conclude that the release had no discernable effect on local cancer rates, alarmist media coverage will energize the anti-nuclear movement both in the United States and around the world.

1982 The Chernobyl plant's reactor #1 suffers a partial core meltdown. Details of the incident are kept secret from the public by the Soviet government.

1983 The last of the Chernobyl plant's four reactors becomes operational.

1985 Anatoly Ivanovich Mayorets, the Soviet Union's Minister of Energy and Electrification, signs an order forbidding nuclear workers from publicly revealing information about nuclear energy's potentially negative effects on people or the environment.

1986 In January, the Chernobyl plant's director, Viktor Bryukhanov, submits a plan, designed by the chief engineer, Nikolai Fomin, to several government agencies for a test of reactor #4; the plan violates some safety rules and bypasses certain critical control features. When Bryukhanov receives no word from Moscow one way or the other, he decides to go ahead with the test anyway.

1986 On April 25, operators at the Chernobyl power plant, under the direction of its deputy chief engineer, Anatoly Dyatlov, begin powering down reactor #4 to prepare for the test. However, a request is made to keep electricity production going until later that night.

1986 Under extreme strain due to disregarded or disconnected safety features, steam channels in reactor #4 erupt, causing a severe thermal explosion (April 26, 1:24 a.m.). This first explosion is followed by several chemical explosions, which in turn destroy the reactor and much of the building in which it is housed, including its roof. As a result, billions of radioactive particles are released into the atmosphere.

1986 On April 27, the evacuation of Pripyat, as well as some nearby farming communities, begins. About 40,000 residents are told to take only what they will need for three days, receiving assurances that they will be returning. Those in charge of the evacuation know this is likely untrue but want to keep panic to a minimum. On April 28, nuclear plant workers in the Swedish town of Forsmark discover abnormally high radiation readings and, after checking their own facility, realize an accident has occurred at Chernobyl.

1986   During April and May firefighters struggle to control the many blazes triggered by the explosions. The last of the fires is extinguished on May 6.

1986   In July Minister Mayorets issues strict orders to his subordinates to maintain complete silence with the media concerning the details of the Chernobyl disaster.

1986   Work is completed in December on the Sarcophagus, a concrete and steel containment structure designed to enclose the damaged reactor and reduce its radioactive emissions.

1987   Six men are put on trial for the Chernobyl disaster, five plant employees and one government official. They are eventually found guilty and sentenced to terms of varying length in a labor camp.

1991   In October a serious fire caused by a faulty electrical device breaks out in the turbine of reactor #2, causing sections of the roof in the turbine hall to come crashing down. In spite of the fact that no radioactive material escapes during the incident, the decision is made to shut down the reactor entirely.

1991   In December the Soviet Union is officialy dissolved as a political entity following the signing of the Belavezha Accords, which in turn gives birth to the Commonwealth of Independent States and grants independence to former Soviet republics.

1993 Seven industrial nations agree to put $700 billion toward the upgrading of RBMK reactors in the former Soviet Union, plus nearly a dozen others of antiquated design.

1994 Russia's own nuclear-safety watchdog agency concludes that its government has been cutting back on safety measures at some of its nuclear power plants — including worker salaries — as a way of dealing with ongoing economic troubles.

1996 Under pressure from the global community the government of Ukraine (now an independent state) agrees to shut down the remaining two reactors at the Chernobyl plant. Reactor #1 is shut down in this year.

2000 When reactor #3 is shut down in December, the Chernobyl plant's service as a provider of electricity ends.

2007 Plans are announced to build a new confinement structure around reactor #4, as the so-called Sarcophagus was designed to last only about thirty years. The new structure, which is scheduled for completion in 2012, is designed to last a hundred years.

Notes

Chapter One

p. 15, "The probability of a large accident may well be vanishingly small . . ."; Stan Openshaw, *Nuclear Power: Siting and Safety*, New York: Routledge, 1983, p. 27.

p. 17, "Scientists prefer to see important tests and experiments . . ."; Daniel F. Ford, *Three Mile Island: Thirty Minutes to Meltdown*, New York: Penguin, 1982, p. 251.

p. 19, "A person determined to make his mark as a leader . . ."; Grigori Medvedev, *The Truth about Chernobyl*, New York: Basic Books, 1991, p. 47.

p. 23, "the operator is required in the written rules . . ."; Richard F. Mould, *Chernobyl: The Real Story*, New York: Pergamon Press, 1988, p. 10.

p. 26, "The lid over the reactor, a thousand-ton concrete disk . . ."; Glenn Alan Cheney, *Chernobyl: The Ongoing Story of the World's Deadliest Nuclear Disaster*, New York: New Discovery, 1993, p. 23.

p. 29, "I was on shift forty metres from the reactor . . ."; Iurii Badaev, quoted in Iurii Shcherbak, *Chernobyl: A Documentary Story*, New York: Saint Martin's Press, 1990, p. 24.

p. 30, "Suddenly I heard a strong burst of steam. . . ."; Unidentified plant worker, quoted in Medvedev, *The Truth about Chernobyl*, pp. 81–82.

Chapter Two

p. 34, "Many critics agree that a nuclear power plant . . ."; Michio Kaku and Jennifer Trainer, *Nuclear Power: Both Sides*, New York: Norton, 1983, p. 83.

p. 37, ". . . in essence, a huge barbed-wire barricade . . .";
Grigori Medvedev, *No Breathing Room: The Aftermath of Chernobyl*, New York: Basic Books, 1993, p. 35.

p. 37, "It must be acknowledged that nuclear power has a brilliant future . . ."; A. M. Petrosyants, quoted in Medvedev, *The Truth about Chernobyl*, p. 3.

p. 38, "You know, it's powerful stuff. . . ."; Lev Naumenko, quoted in Medvedev, *No Breathing Room*, p. 42.

p. 38, "There was a conspiracy of silence . . ."; Medvedev, *The Truth about Chernobyl*, p. 39.

Chapter Three

p. 41, "I rushed off along the usual route . . ."; Iurii Badaev, quoted in Shcherbak, *Chernobyl: A Documentary Story*, 1990, p. 25.

p. 42, "At his feet there were some smoldering lumps . . ."; Piers Paul Read, *Ablaze: The Story of the Heroes and Victims of Chernobyl*, New York: Random House, 1993, p. 70.

p. 43, "Bryukhanov had followed the standard Soviet protocol . . ."; W. Scott Ingram, *The Chernobyl Nuclear Disaster*, New York: Facts on File, 2005, p. 49.

p. 43, "We didn't have much idea about radiation . . ."; Hryhorii Khmel, quoted in Shcherbak, *Chernobyl*, p. 33.

p. 45, "They told us it would be for three days . . ."; L. Kovaleska, quoted in Shcherbak, *Chernobyl*, p. 64.

p. 46, "From the point of view of the civil defense . . ."; Read, *Ablaze*, p. 103.

p. 46, "One side of the street there are buses . . ."; Lyudmilla Ignatenko, quoted in Svetlana Alexievich, *Voices from*

Chernobyl: The Oral History of a Nuclear Disaster, Normal, IL: Dalkey Archive Press, 2005, p. 8.

p. 47, "All morning I had been doing the laundry . . ."; Lyudmila Kharitonova, quoted in Medvedev, *The Truth about Chernobyl*, 1991, pp. 137–138.

p. 49, ". . . clear that the officials in Moscow did not understand . . ."; Zhores Medvedev, *The Legacy of Chernobyl*, New York: Norton, 1990, p. 50.

p. 54, "When an incident has cross-border implications . . ."; George Shultz, quoted in John Greenwald, "Deadly Meltdown," *Time*, May 12, 1986.

p. 54, "The Soviets owe the world an explanation . . ."; Ronald Reagan, Radio Address to the Nation on the President's Trip to Indonesia and Japan, May 4, 1986, quoted in John Wolley and Gerhard Peters, "The American Presidency Project," www.presidency.ucsb.edu/ws/index.php ?pid=37208.

p. 54, ". . . were furious with the Soviets for initially concealing . . ."; Greenwald, "Deadly Meltdown."

p. 56, "We can understand an accident. . . ."; unnamed Warsaw resident, quoted in Greenwald, "Deadly Meltdown."

p. 56, "There is no sense of a growing crisis here . . ."; Noriaki Hosokawa, quoted in John Greenwald, "More Fallout from Chernobyl," *Time*, May 19, 1986.

p. 57, "We take water from lochs and streams . . ."; Alan Rutherford, quoted in Greenwald, "More Fallout from Chernobyl."

p. 57, "We have discussed the implications of the accident . . ."; Group statement by G7 leaders, . . . quoted in Philippe

J. Sands, *Chernobyl: Law and Communication*, Cambridge, UK: Grotius, 1988, p. 222.

p. 57, "Alexsandr Petrovskii and I went up onto the roof . . ."; Ivan Shavrei, quoted in Mould, *Chernobyl: The Real Story*, 1988, p. 60.

p. 59, "We were between twenty-five and forty [years old] . . ."; Arkady Filin, quoted in Alexievich, *Voices from Chernobyl*, pp. 87–88.

Chapter Four

p. 67, "I'm asking why you have been giving Medvedev information . . ."; soviet official, quoted in Medvedev, *No Breathing Room:* p. 124.

p. 68, "The lead that helicopters dropped . . ."; Glenn Alan Cheney, *Journey to Chernobyl: Encounters in a Radioactive Zone*, Chicago: Academy Chicago, 1995, p. 48.

p. 73, ". . . was born just two years after the Chernobyl disaster . . ."; Linda Walker, *Living after Chernobyl: Ira's Story*. Milwaukee: World Almanac Library, 2006, pp. 8–9.

p. 76, "What they're dealing with is a syndrome . . ."; quoted in Cheney, *Journey to Chernobyl*, pp. 75–76.

p. 76, "I have every reason to say that, despite the utter gravity . . ."; text of television address by Mikhail Gorbachev given May 14, 1986, quoted in Mould, *Chernobyl: The Real Story*, 1988, p. 197.

p. 77, "Chernobyl soils are quite suitable for seeding . . ."; Dmitri Grodzinski, quoted in Read, *Ablaze: The Story of the Heroes and Victims of Chernobyl*, p. 267.

p. 80, "With so many human deaths, I cannot say . . ."; Anatoly Dyatlov, quoted in John Greenwald and Ken Olsen, "Disaster Judgment at Chernobyl," *Time*, July 20, 1987.

p. 80, ". . . atmosphere of lack of control . . ."; Raimond Brize, quoted in William J. Eaton, "Six Guilty in Chernobyl Blast—Sentenced to Labor Camps," *Los Angeles Times*, July 29, 1987.

Chapter Five

p. 83, "United Nations nuclear and health watchdogs . . ."; John Vidal, "UN Accused of Ignoring 500,000 Chernobyl Deaths," *Guardian*, March 25, 2006.

p. 84, "Because all sources of energy based on fire are limited . . ."; Zhores Medvedev, *The Legacy of Chernobyl*, New York: Norton, 1990, p. 312.

p. 85, "When a brigade of Greenpeace activists . . ."; Anthony Faiola, "Nuclear Power Regains Support," *Washington Post*, November 24, 2009.

p. 85, "Expects also point to a host of improvements . . ."; Faiola, "Nuclear Power Regains Support."

p. 86, "Every year there are thousands of incidents. . . ."; Georgui Kastchiev et al., "Residual Risk: An Account of Events in Nuclear Power Plants since the Chernobyl Accident in 1986," report commissioned by the European Parliament, May 2007, p. 3.

p. 91, "I want to bear witness . . ."; in Alexievich, *Voices from Chernobyl*, p. 36.

Further Information

Books

Heinrichs, Ann. *Sustaining Earth's Energy Resources*. New York: Marshall Cavendish Benchmark, 2011.

Kanninen, Barbara. *Atomic Energy*. Farmington Hills, MI: Greenhaven Press, 2005.

McLeish, Ewan. *The Pros and Cons of Nuclear Power*. New York: Rosen, 2007.

Walker, Linda. *Children in Crisis: Living after Chernobyl—Ira's Story*. Milwaukee: World Almanac Library, 2005.

DVDs

History of Nuclear Energy: Problems and Promises. Orlando, FL: A2ZCDS, 2005.

History of Nuclear Power: Power and the People. Orlando, FL: A2ZCDS, 2006.

Websites

Chernobyl Accident

www.world-nuclear.org/info/chernobyl/inf07.html

This page within the World Nuclear Association site contains a great many facts on the Chernobyl accident and goes into extensive detail. Links to other sites are also included. This nicely presented and well-maintained page also allows students to acquire basic information about nuclear power by navigating through the many pull-down menus.

Energy Kids: Uranium (Nuclear) Basics

www.eia.doe.gov/kids/energyfacts/sources/non-renewable/
nuclear.html

This page, from the U.S. government's Energy Information
Administration (EIA) website, covers basic topics within the
field of nuclear energy: uranium, reactors, generators, fission
and fusion, how these and other aspects of nuclear power
affect the environment, and many others.

Nuclear Energy

www.worldalmanacforkids.com/WAKI-ViewArticle.aspx
?pin=x-nu067100a&article_id=186&chapter_id=4&chapter_
title=Environment&article_title=Nuclear_Energy

The nuclear energy page on the World Almanac for Kids
site is a bit more advanced and incorporates more detail on
all aspects of the production of nuclear power than the
EIA's Energy Kids page. Also included here is good basic
information on the Chernobyl and Three Mile Island
incidents.

Bibliography

Alexievich, Svetlana. *Voices from Chernobyl: The Oral History of a Nuclear Disaster*. Normal, IL: Dalkey Archive Press, 2005.

Cheney, Glenn Alan. *Chernobyl: The Ongoing Story of the World's Deadliest Nuclear Disaster*. New York: New Discovery, 1993.

———. *Journey to Chernobyl: Encounters in a Radioactive Zone*. Chicago: Academy Chicago, 1995.

Eaton, William J. "Six Go on Trial in Chernobyl Disaster — Former Chief of Nuclear Plant, Five Aides Face Prison Terms." *Los Angeles Times*, July 8, 1987.

———. "Six Guilty in Chernobyl Blast — Sentenced to Labor Camps." *Los Angeles Times*, July 29, 1987.

Faiola, Anthony. "Nuclear Power Regains Support." *Washington Post*, November 24, 2009.

Ford, Daniel F. *Meltdown: The Secret Papers of the Atomic Energy Commission*. New York: Touchstone, 1986.

———. *Three Mile Island: Thirty Minutes to Meltdown*. New York: Penguin, 1982.

Greenwald, John. "Deadly Meltdown." *Time*, May 12, 1986.

———. "More Fallout from Chernobyl." *Time*, May 19, 1986.

Greenwald, John, and Ken Olsen. "Disaster Judgment at Chernobyl." *Time*, July 20, 1987.

Ingram, W. Scott. *The Chernobyl Nuclear Disaster*. New York: Facts on File, 2005.

Kaku, Michio, and Jennifer Trainer. *Nuclear Power: Both Sides*. New York: Norton, 1983.

Kastchiev, Georgui, et al. "Residual Risk: An Account of Events in Nuclear Power Plants since the Chernobyl Accident in 1986." Report commissioned by the European Parliament, May 2007.

Medvedev, Grigori. *No Breathing Room: The Aftermath of Chernobyl*. New York: Basic Books, 1993.

——. *The Truth about Chernobyl*. New York: Basic Books, 1991.

Medvedev, Zhores. *The Legacy of Chernobyl*. New York: Norton, 1990.

Mould, Richard F. *Chernobyl: The Real Story*. New York: Pergamon Press, 1988.

Openshaw, Stan. *Nuclear Power: Siting and Safety*. New York: Routledge, 1983.

Read, Piers Paul. *Ablaze: The Story of the Heroes and Victims of Chernobyl*. New York: Random House, 1993.

Sands, Philippe J. *Chernobyl: Law and Communication*, Cambridge, UK: Grotius, 1988.

Shcherbak, Iurii. *Chernobyl: A Documentary Story*. New York: Saint Martin's Press, 1990.

Vidal, John. "UN Accused of Ignoring 500,000 Chernobyl Deaths." *Guardian*, March 25, 2006.

Walker, Linda. *Living after Chernobyl: Ira's Story*. Milwaukee: World Almanac Library, 2006.

Index

Page numbers in **boldface** are illustrations.

About the Author

WIL MARA is the award-winning author of more than one hundred books. He has written both fiction and nonfiction for children and adults. More information about his work can be found at www.wilmara.com.